Seven Wonders Of The Faith

*Answers To Our
Most Troubling Questions*

Charles D. Reeb

CSS Publishing Company, Inc., Lima, Ohio

SEVEN WONDERS OF THE FAITH

Copyright © 2006 by
CSS Publishing Company, Inc.
Lima, Ohio

All rights reserved. No part of this publication may be reproduced in any manner whatsoever without the prior permission of the publisher, except in the case of brief quotations embodied in critical articles and reviews. Inquiries should be addressed to: Permissions, CSS Publishing Company, Inc., 517 South Main Street, Lima, Ohio 45804.

Scripture quotations are from the New Revised Standard Version of the Bible, copyright 1989 by the Division of Christian Education of the National Council of the Churches of Christ in the USA. Used by permission.

Library of Congress Cataloging-in-Publication Data

Reeb, Charles D., 1973-
　Seven wonders of the faith : answers to our most troubling questions / Charles D. Reeb.
　　p. cm.
　ISBN 0-7880-2418-3 (perfect bound : alk paper)
　1. Apologetics. I. Title.

BT1103.R44 2006
239—dc22

2006020298

For more information about CSS Publishing Company resources, visit our website at www.csspub.com or email us at custserv@csspub.com or call (800) 241-4056.

Cover design by Barbara Spencer
ISBN-13: 978-0-7880-2418-7
ISBN-10: 0-7880-2418-3   PRINTED IN U.S.A.

*To my mother, Jane Reeb,
who encouraged me to wonder
and showed me where to find truth*

Table Of Contents

Foreword	7
Chapter One I Wonder If God Exists	9
Chapter Two I Wonder Why Bad Things Happen To Good People	17
Chapter Three I Wonder Why My Prayers Go Unanswered	23
Chapter Four I Wonder About God's Will For My Life	29
Chapter Five I Wonder About The Miracles In The Bible	35
Chapter Six I Wonder About The End Of The World	39
Chapter Seven I Wonder About Life After Death	45

Foreword

Recently, the Barna Research Group conducted an important poll to get the pulse of inquiring hearts about religion. They asked a cross section of American adults: "If you could ask God any question about your life, what is the single most important question you would want to ask him?"[1] In addition, *USA Today* conducted a similar poll by asking readers, "If you could get in contact with God directly, and get an immediate reply, what would you ask?"[2] Not surprisingly, the results of these polls yielded very similar results. Many of the questions had to do with suffering, life purpose, life after death, the end of the world, and God's will. I believe it is a safe assumption that those who choose to read this book also have questions that fall under these categories.

Many people feel ashamed for having doubts and questions about their faith. They fear that they will be accused of not trusting God enough or being spiritually immature. Often there are people of faith who are eager to criticize those who dare to question God. This is unfortunate, for there is more faith in doubt than most realize. In fact, if you study the lives of great Christians throughout history, you will find that many of them (including biblical writers) went through profound periods of doubting and questioning God and their faith. They came out of their period of searching with a stronger faith and a deeper understanding of God. Honest doubts and questions of faith are not only about finding answers, but also about discovering truth.

The following sermons speak to common questions of faith that many of us ask. They were born out of my own heart, as well as the hearts of those whom I am privileged to serve as pastor. They were originally preached as a sermon series to a congregation, which, like many others, was seeking answers to troubling questions of faith. Three of the sermons were also preached on *Day 1* (formerly known as *The Protestant Hour*). It is my prayer that these sermons in their present form will now assist clergy and laity in seeking truth through questions of "ultimate concern."

Charles D. Reeb

1. Woodrow Kroll, *An Interview with God* (Chicago: Moody Publishers, 2004).

2. "Going to a Higher Authority," *USA Today*, 28 May 1999.

Chapter One

I Wonder If God Exists

The conversation was going well. I respected my new friend's intellectual prowess. He seemed to be able to speak intelligently on every subject. When we got to the subject of religion, he said quite casually, "I can't believe in God." Knowing the difference between head knowledge and heart knowledge, I replied, "You mean, you can't bring yourself to follow him?" "No," he retorted, "I mean, I really can't believe that God exists. How can anyone believe in God when the world is as messed up as it is? I could do a better job creating and running a universe." His words reminded me of the old line by Woody Allen, "If there is a God, he is the ultimate under-achiever."

As a pastor, many of my conversations with people about God begin in this manner. I will be on a plane or sitting in a waiting room and as soon as people discover that I am "a man of the cloth," they express their inability to wrap their minds around the existence of God. I take them seriously because many want to believe in God, but they can't seem to get over their intellectual hurdles. They desire to be convinced that God exists, but their rationale for not believing in God will not relent. Their god is what can be observed and studied.

Of course, not all of the people I speak with about the existence of God are so convinced in one way or the other. Many call themselves agnostics, and, as such, just aren't sure what they believe. Some waiver back and forth on whether or not God exists. Others believe in God, but they are not sure about the nature of God. Is God loving or hateful? Does God care about the world or has God abandoned us? They study world religions and it just confuses them more. In addition, many of them look to the behavior of those who claim to believe in God and are not impressed with what they find. This is a sobering indictment on the church.

When I speak with Christians about the existence of God, surprisingly, many are not able to articulate reasons why they believe in the existence of a benevolent being who created the universe and is active in the world today. For them, it is an issue of faith, as it should be. However, when they find themselves in conversations with people who have serious doubts about the existence of God many are unable to "to make their defense" (1 Peter 3:15) as to why they believe in the reality of God. Some are left with the same doubts as those who don't believe. Their faith is challenged.

Most of you who are reading these words probably can identify with one or all of the people above. All of us, at one time or another, have wondered about the existence of God. This is the reason for this chapter. Some want legitimate arguments for the existence of God to help bring them to faith in God. Others desire clear and concise explanations for God's existence in order to feel prepared when articulating the reason for their beliefs when they are challenged. My prayer is that what follows will satisfy your requests.

Everything Begins With God

People have been wondering about God's existence since there has been a human being on earth who could reflect on the meaning of life. The question of the reality of God goes to the core of human existence. For most people, what they believe about God determines what they believe about their lives and how they should live. In other words, their belief in God determines their behavior. Of course, there will always be folks who are "practical atheists" — they believe in God but they act as if there were no God. However, for many, values and morals have their root in a belief in God. If God exists, life matters. If God doesn't exist, we are left to our own devices with truth being a relative idea depending upon the whims of culture. Those who believe in God feel that without God there is no morality, no goodness, and no absolute truth, for God is the source of all these things.

The Bible Does Not Prove The Existence Of God

The Bible does not set out to prove the existence of God. If we turn to the first page of the Bible we read, "In the beginning ... God" (Genesis 1:1). There is no attempt to convince the reader that

God exists. The Bible clearly assumes that there is a God. God simply is. Psalm 14:1 says, "Fools say in their hearts, 'There is no God.' " From a biblical perspective, what is obvious and certain does not need to be proven.

However, many people do not feel that the reality of God is so obvious. To atheists it seems clear that there is not a God, and many are very vocal about it. To agnostics the jury is still out on the whole issue of God, and even if they are convinced that God exists, they are not sure what this divine being is up to. Yet, I believe clear reflection on the arguments for God's existence brings the obvious to bear.

There are many compelling and convincing arguments for the existence of God. Scholars, philosophers, and theologians have used them within academia for years. Many of these arguments are known within Christian theology as *general revelation*, which means that they are based on what is generally known and observable. Unfortunately, these arguments for God's existence typically do not get mentioned within churches. Some religious leaders feel that attempting to explain these arguments will just bring more confusion to the average layperson. I disagree. Those who seek for the reality of God need and deserve the most compelling evidence for God's existence. What follows is a summary of some of the best arguments for the existence of God.

The Design Argument

One of the most compelling arguments for the existence of God is what is often called "the design argument." Many people have reasoned out this argument on their own without realizing that it has a name or an official distinction. Set out by philosopher William Paley, this simple argument is also known as "Paley's Watch." Basically, the argument goes that if you happened upon a watch, never having seen a watch or heard of one and you broke it open to look at its intricate parts, you would conclude that this watch was made by a watchmaker. In the same way, the world we observe is too complex and too beautiful to have happened by chance. The world must have been created and designed by a divine intelligence.

Many of us have had the experience that Paley reasoned out. We observe a beautiful tree, flower, or mountain, and exclaim, "Only God could have created that!" The psalmist was expressing the design argument when he said, "I praise you for I am fearfully and wonderfully made. Wonderful are your works; that I know very well" (Psalm 139:14). Just a glance at the beauty around us and the wonder of our working bodies and we are compelled to conclude that there is a God who is behind everything.

Those who are still not convinced should consider the probability of the world coming together by mere chance. According to what we know from science and biology, the world existing by chance would be as if a tornado had touched down in a junkyard, rearranged all of the parts, and left a fully operational Boeing 747 in its wake. This incomprehensible event wouldn't have to happen only once, it would have to happen a million times! Such an event is clearly impossible, and so is the creation of the world without a designer.[1]

The First Cause Argument

Another convincing argument for the existence of God is known as the "first cause argument." It is sometimes referred to as the "cosmological argument." Most believe this argument began with Saint Thomas Aquinas, who sought to discover the cause for the origin of our world. The first part to this argument states that every event has a cause (nothing comes from nothing). For instance, this book you hold in your hands did not just appear out of thin air; it was put together by a publisher. Aquinas believed that if we go back far enough we can find the first event which is the "first cause" for all the subsequent events.

The second part to Aquinas' argument is that things move because they are moved by something else. The balls on a pool table move because they are struck by other balls. If you trace all movement you will discover an *unmoved mover* who is independent of all moves and causes. Aquinas argued that the ultimate cause of all events and movements is God.

The Moral Argument

Perhaps the most obvious argument for the existence of God is the "moral argument." This argument states quite simply that our sense of right and wrong comes from God. For example, we know that trying to save a person from drowning is right and throwing someone incapable of swimming into a lake is wrong. Right and wrong seem to be fundamental; they don't have to be taught. We know what "ought" to be done. Some call this innate knowledge of right and wrong our conscience. Where does our conscience come from? Our conscience does not originate with us; it comes from God.

If there is no God, then human beings decide what is right and wrong and no moral code is fixed. People would behave based upon what feels good or what is right for them, and the world would be in utter chaos. There is a God because God is the only logical source and commander of what is right and wrong.

The Existence Of Religion

A less known, but no less important, argument for God's existence is the reality of religion in our world. A cursory study of history will show that religion has played a vital role in every human culture. Even indigenous tribes who live in the most remote areas of the world have some sort of religion. There seems to be an innate desire for human beings to worship something bigger than themselves. This desire could only come from God. We are designed to be connected to our Creator, so we will naturally express what we're designed by God to do.

Saint Augustine once prayed to God, "Our hearts are restless until they rest in thee." The prominence of religion in our world underscores Augustine's prayer. There truly is a "God-shaped void in all of us that only God can fill."

The Significance Of Jesus Christ

After reading these arguments, skeptics may be inclined to believe in some sort of "higher power" or divine force. However, these arguments fall short in proving the nature of God. For instance, we may be able to believe that God created the world, but what does it say about this God when there is a natural disaster or when people are born into this world with severe mental and physical disorders? How can we be sure that we are dealing with a benevolent God that so many people believe in? Or what about people who worship many gods or different religions that are in conflict over the nature of God and how God operates in the world? What kind of God are we to believe in? How are we to know what this "higher power" is like?

Enter Jesus Christ. Because we are limited and finite human beings who can never fully understand and know God on our own, we need God to come down to our level and exemplify his nature. This is what God does in Jesus Christ. In Christ, God demonstrates for us what he is like and proves his redeeming love toward us by dying on a cross. The birth, ministry, death, and resurrection of Jesus Christ make God's nature and power real for us in a way that we can understand. More importantly, through Christ we encounter this loving God and are redeemed from sin and given new life.

In most religions, human beings are reaching for God. Only the Christian faith claims that God reaches for us. In Christ, an invisible God penetrates our world and transforms our lives. God's revelation to us in Jesus Christ is so significant that it is called *special revelation*. Unlike *general revelation*, special revelation is God's particular and deliberate act of revealing his love to us. This is the reason many theologians argue that when talking about God we must begin with Christ, for in Christ we experience the true nature of God.

The Best Argument For God

The best argument for the existence of God is not some philosophical idea or a brilliant conclusion reached by the foremost theologian. The most compelling and convincing argument for God is personal experience. Bruce Shelley reinforces this point when he writes about trying to prove that poetry exists. Shelley mentions that some could argue that poetry is nothing more than black marks on white paper. This argument might be convincing for folks who cannot read or hear. In fact, after examining print under a microscope and analyzing the paper and ink, you would never find anything that could be called poetry. However, those who can read or hear poetry and experience it will insist that poetry exists.

It is the same way with God. We can throw philosophical darts back and forth, arguing about God's existence. But it is only when we allow ourselves to experience God's redeeming love in Jesus Christ that we truly believe and are changed. The point is that we come to faith in God not head first, but heart first. We may intellectually believe that God exists, but it only makes a difference when we give him our hearts. God spoke through the prophet Jeremiah and said, "When you search for me, you will find me; if you seek me with all of your heart" (29:13).

Do you really want to know if God exists? Give God your heart and ask him to cleanse you of all your sins and put a new spirit within you. Once you experience God's redeeming love, your question will no longer be, "Does God exist?" but "How did I exist without God in my life?"

---

1. Ryan Roberts, *Does the Big Bang Prove The Existence of God?* (University of Calgary, Alberta), p. 10 (www.Halozone.Com).

Chapter Two

I Wonder Why Bad Things Happen To Good People*

As we remember the terror of 9/11, we long for answers. As we experience pain in our lives, our hearts cry out. As we continue to face the difficulties and challenges of life, our minds seek satisfaction to this enigma. It is the age-old puzzle that haunts us: "I wonder why bad things happen to good people." This is a burning question for anyone who has experienced the horrors of life. Churches are flooded with people asking this question. Counselors are overbooked with clients asking this question. People all over the world pray this question: Why do bad things happen to good people? The brokenness of life shatters many people's ideas about how the world is supposed to operate.

We don't live life very long before many of our illusions are shattered. I recall a cartoon that appeared in *The Atlanta Constitution* after a man named Mark Barton walked into an Atlanta business office then shot and killed several people. In the cartoon, a small boy is sitting next to his mother and a newspaper is lying on the table. The headline reads, "Atlanta Murderer: Mark Barton." Confused, the boy is looking up at his mother saying, "You said monsters don't exist."[1] We are all like that boy, and we ask about this monster in many ways: "Why do the innocent suffer and the wicked prosper?" "Why does God allow evil and suffering?" "If God is great and good, why is there suffering?" Another way it is put is: "If God can't stop suffering, then he is not great. If he can, then he is not good." In the study of theology this wonder is called the *theodicy question*, and it has been asked since the very beginning of recorded history.

A Biblical Question

It may come as a surprise to some that the theodicy question can be seen throughout the Bible. The Psalms ask it. Job asks it. Lamentations is full of it. The prophet Habakkuk complains to God about it. The prophet Jeremiah questions God about it: Why do the wicked prosper and the innocent suffer? We ought to take a lesson from the biblical writers who cry out with this same burning question that we ask today. The lesson is that if we are going to be intimate and personal with God, we need to give him all that we have inside of us, even our deepest complaints and questions. Don't worry. God is big enough to handle them!

It may be some consolation that the Bible asks the theodicy question, but is there an answer? Unfortunately, there is not an answer, at least not one that would satisfy most of us. The simple fact is that the Bible asks the question, but it never completely answers it. Deuteronomy 29:29 says, "The secret things belong to the Lord our God." This side of heaven we will never know why bad things happen to good people.

The Evil Side Of Free Will

There is an incomplete response to the theodicy question: free will. God wants us to love him because we choose to love him, so he has given us free will. It is a great gift, but there is a negative side to it. People can use their free will to do evil things and cause much pain and suffering. So, on 9/11/01, certain people chose to use their free will to get into airplanes, crash into buildings, and kill innocent people.

However, free will is an incomplete response to the theodicy question because it does not address things like natural disasters and various diseases — those things that human beings do not cause to happen. The truth is that we live in a sinful world that runs amok and bad things happen to both the innocent and the guilty.

As Christians, we believe that one day Christ will come in glory and all of our questions will be answered, all of the great mysteries will be solved, and all of our confusion will turn into clarity. So get your list of questions ready for that day. I know I've got mine! And the question at the top of my list will be, "Why did bad things happen to good people?"

You know what Mother Teresa said? She said, "When I die, God will have a lot of answering to do." Billy Graham also said, "When I die and go to heaven, I will spend the first 100 years just asking God questions." We can look forward to doing the same thing.

Until that great day comes, however, we still have to cope with life in all of its suffering and tragedy. We still have to deal with the bad and unfair circumstances of life. So, I want to offer some things that have helped me as I have struggled with the question of why bad things happen to good people. My prayer is that they will help you, too.

Don't Become Cynical

The first bit of help I offer is simply this: Do not allow the theodicy question to make you cynical. It's fair and healthy to ask this question and struggle with it, but I have seen too many people hang on to it way too long, like a protest, and remain stuck in their faith, or stop believing in God altogether. I have also seen people use it as an excuse. Some feel that as long as they wear a badge of prideful agnosticism, they will not have to deal with the truth of God in their lives.

Don't allow unfair pain and suffering to harden your heart. A good way to protect yourself from cynicism is to reflect on the insightful words of Harry Emerson Fosdick: "Goodness is a far greater problem for the atheist than evil is for the believer." Instead of focusing on the evil and suffering in the world, look at all the goodness that abounds! Where does all this goodness come from? It can only come from a loving God who cares for us. Allow the goodness in the world to lead you back to the goodness of God.

A Better Question

I believe the best help I can give as we grapple with the question of why bad things happen to good people is to offer another question: What happens to good people when bad things happen to them? This is a question that the Bible does answer. In the eighth chapter of Romans, Paul uses several words to describe the pain and suffering of life: hardship, persecution, distress, nakedness, famine, peril, and the sword (v. 35). Paul and the early Christians were very much in touch with unfair suffering. But what did Paul say happens to us when we experience bad things? Not only did he say that we will never be separated from God's love, but in Romans 8:28 Paul says something truly remarkable: "We know that all things work together for good for those who love God, who are called according to his purpose."

This remarkable verse expresses that evil and pain are never the will of God, but God can take evil and pain and use them for good. Over and over again in life we see this. When evil attacks with pain, God uses it to build character. When evil shows resistance, God uses it to build strength. When evil cripples with tragedy, God finds a way to victory. When evil destroys with death, God restores life. God is in the transformation business. God can turn our trouble into triumph!

One of the greatest examples of God turning rough times into glory is the story of Joseph in Genesis. Joseph was the favored son and his brothers were jealous. In a jealous rage they beat him and sold him into slavery as a youth. Through an amazing turn of events, as Joseph grew older, his abilities impressed the authorities of Egypt and the Pharaoh made him second in command in Egypt!

Joseph had the power to get revenge on his brothers, but he didn't. Instead, he forgave them. His brothers approached him, scared to death, and Joseph said, "Don't be afraid. Am I God? I can't judge you. What you did was meant to hurt me, but God used it for good. I have strength and character, and now I have the power to save and provide for the people of Israel." At that moment Joseph knew that God had taken something very ugly and made it beautiful.

It Is Well With Our Souls
H. G. Spafford had the same experience. In 1873, his wife and four children sailed from New York to France on an ocean liner. Mr. Spafford was unable to make the voyage with his family because of business commitments in Chicago. He told them "Goodbye," promising to meet them in France in a few weeks.

At two o'clock on the morning of November 22, 1873, when the luxury liner was several days out, it was hit by another liner. Within two hours, the ship sank. Nine days later when the survivors landed at Cardiff, Wales, Mrs. Spafford cabled her husband these two words, "Saved alone." When he received her message, he quickly booked passage on a ship to Europe to join his wife. On the way over, the captain called him into his cabin and said, "I believe we are now passing over the place where your family's liner went down."

That night in the mid-Atlantic, filled with much pain and sorrow, Mr. Spafford wrote five stanzas, the first of which contained these lines: "When peace like a river attendeth my way, When sorrows like sea-billows roll, Whatever my lot, Thou hast taught me to say, It is well, it is well with my soul!"[2] These familiar words have been a part of one of the most popular hymns in the church today. Little did Spafford know that his words would give comfort to so many people. God turned his scar into a star.

We can't control the fact that bad things will happen to us. They just do, and one day we will find out why. But the one thing we can control is how we respond to the bad things that happen to us. We can get bitter or better! We can stay angry at life and at God and never move on, or we can give our pain to God and allow him to do something beautiful with it. If we choose what God can do through our pain, we will be able to say with confidence:

> *I will be untouched in the midst of fire*
> *I will stand firm in the midst of a storm*
> *I will not crack in the midst of chaos*
> *I will not lose heart when the world is torn*
>
> *I will not fear when the heat blazes*
> *I will not fret when drought comes*
> *I will bear fruit in the midst of all of it*
> *I will march to a different drum*
>
> *I will discover victory in tragedy*
> *I will trust in El Shaddai*
> *I will laugh in the face of death*
> *I will wave evil and pain good-bye*
> — Charles D. Reeb

---

*Sermon aired on *Day 1* on September 11, 2005 (www.day1.net).

1. Cartoon by Mike Lukovich of *The Atlanta Constitution.*

2. Words by Horatio G. Spafford, 1873, in public domain.

Chapter Three

I Wonder Why My Prayers Go Unanswered*

Warren Wiersbe tells of the time when he was helping to paint the outside of his neighbors' home. His neighbors had a small black dog that had a ritual of going to the back door of the house. Once the little dog took up his station at the back door, he would bark and bark until someone finally got the message and let him out.

One day Wiersbe was painting the outside of the house when no one was home. The neighbor's dog started his ritual at the back door and barked and barked all day long. The sad thing, Wiersbe said, was that it never dawned in his little brain that all his barking was totally useless — no one was home to hear!

Perhaps many of you feel like that dog. You have prayed and prayed for something and there seems to be no answer — there seems to be no one home! And maybe you are beginning to have this nagging wonder about why your prayers are going unanswered.

You are not alone! Throughout scripture we see examples of followers of God who cried out and did not seem to have their prayers answered. The two biggest examples are Jesus and Paul. Remember, Jesus pled for God to take the "cup" of sacrifice from him, but to no avail. And the Apostle Paul begged God to take away the thorn in his flesh, but God never did. Obviously, their prayers were not answered to their satisfaction.

We can receive comfort from the fact that even Jesus and Paul went through times of fervent praying for God to do something and God not complying with their requests. We are not alone with what seems like our unanswered prayers.

What Is Prayer?

Perhaps you are thinking, "Wait a second, didn't Jesus tell us that if we ask, seek, and knock, we will receive an answer?" (Luke 11:9-10). Yes. That is what he said, and his words are true, but we must first understand what prayer is before we can understand the truth and power of Jesus' words. Prayer is one of the most misunderstood and misused practices of our faith, and until we understand the nature of prayer, all of our barking and praying for an answer will leave us frustrated. Our wondering about unanswered prayer is often due to a misunderstanding about the nature of prayer.

For many, prayer is understood as an exercise in magic. There are a number of popular religious books out there that seem to support this. People often believe that if they say the right phrases or have the proper technique, they can persuade God to answer their prayers.

There is an old story of a monk who was bothered by mice playing around him when he prayed. To stop it, he got a cat and kept it in his prayer room so the mice would be scared away. However, he never explained to his disciples why he had the cat. One day the monk walked down the corridors of the monastery and noticed that each of his disciples had a cat in their prayer room. After seeing the monk with a cat, they thought having a cat was the secret to powerful praying!

This is a parable for many Christians today. Many believe they have to do something special in order for God to hear them and have their prayers answered. You will often see folks running here and there to learn the latest prayer gimmick from self-proclaimed spiritual gurus.

Prayer is not rubbing a magic lamp. It is not presenting some Santa Claus in the sky with a list of things we want. Prayer is intimate communication with our Lord. It is as natural as turning around and speaking to a friend. More importantly, it is being quiet and still and listening to God and being transformed by what he is communicating to us. Prayer is vital, for how can we expect to be in relationship with God if we don't communicate with God?

The Prayer Life Of Jesus

Jesus taught us what prayer is by his own example. Just read through the Gospel of Luke, and you will find Jesus praying consistently at every turn in his life. He prays as he senses God's call in his life, he prays before choosing his disciples, and he prays as he serves and heals other people. He prays as he feels the demands and pressures of his ministry, he prays as he faces the cross, and he prays as he finishes his work on the cross. Jesus is continually praying. You could say that prayer for him was as vital as taking his next breath. He knew that in order to live out the life God called him to live, he needed to be continually connected to God in prayer; God was the source of his power.

It was out of his own consistent prayer life that Jesus gives us the teaching we find in Luke 11. The disciples notice Jesus praying frequently, and they finally get a clue and say, "Teach us to pray." They observe that prayer is a vital practice for Jesus and they want to learn how to do it. What follows is a profound lesson from Jesus about prayer. However, notice that it is not a lesson in right technique. It is not a lesson in right phrasing. It is not a lesson in how to persuade God. It is a lesson in persistence. Through the story of the man banging on the door all night, and the repeated words, ask, seek, and knock, Jesus is telling us that effective prayer is consistent prayer. Effective prayer is a continual connection to God.

If we look closely at Luke 11 and the prayer that Jesus gave us, we will also notice Jesus told us what is perhaps the most important lesson about prayer. Effective prayer is not about what we can get from God, but what we receive from God. There is a big difference! Often times, what we want from God and what we receive from God are two different things.

Don't Like The Answer?

Perhaps this changes your wondering about unanswered prayer. Maybe God has answered you and you just don't like the answer. Someone once said that God answers prayer in one of four ways: yes, no, wait, and are you kidding? This is somewhat glib, but there is some truth to it. I recall times in my own life when I prayed and prayed for God to give me something, and my prayers were never answered, or so I thought. Later, I discovered that what I wanted was not right for me. That event always reminds me of the country song, "Thank God For Unanswered Prayer."

There have been other times when God seemed to know that I was not ready for the answer to my prayer or the timing was not right, and God asked me to wait. It was then that I relied on the words of the psalmist: "Wait on the Lord" (Psalm 27:14).

We need to keep in mind that what is implied in Jesus' words recorded in Luke's Gospel is that God always answers prayer. God may not give us the answer we want or answer us at the time we desire, but God always answers us. And God will always answer us with our best interest at heart. Remember, Jesus said: "If you then, who are evil, know how to give good gifts to your children, how much more will the heavenly Father give the Holy Spirit to those who ask him?" (Luke 11:13). This is a great promise that should encourage us to pray more!

Notice what Jesus does not say. He does not say, "How much more will the Heavenly Father give you what you want when you ask for it?" He says that those who ask him will be given the *Holy Spirit*. This means that when we pray, God gives us what we need to be empowered and to grow.

Prayer Changes Things

I remember playing with the pew pencils in church when I was a kid. The pencils always had these words inscribed on them: "Prayer Changes Things." As I have grown in my faith, I have learned that prayer does indeed "change things," but it is not God who changes. It is me. There is a wonderful old phrase: *"Prayer does not give us what we want, but prayer helps us want what we need."* How true that is. You see, prayer is not designed to change or persuade God; it is designed by God to change us! Prayer is a spiritual discipline through which we are formed into disciples of Jesus Christ.

In his classic book, *The Meaning of Prayer*, Harry Emerson Fosdick puts it this way: "Some things God cannot give to a person until he has prepared and proved his spirit by persistent prayer. Such praying cleans the house, cleanses the windows, hangs the curtains, sets the table, opens the door, until God says, 'Lo! The house is ready. Now may the guest come in.'"

I believe this is what Jesus is driving at in his teaching about prayer in Luke. When we ask long enough, seek hard enough, knock loud enough, and pray persistently enough, something happens inside us. The discipline of prayer begins to awaken us to the Holy Spirit within, and our motives and desires begin to change. It is as though the persistence of our praying becomes the axe that breaks up the frozen numbness of our souls. The power and wisdom of God break in and we begin to be formed by the will of God.

Peter Annet once said that those who pray persistently are like sailors who have cast anchor on a rock. As they pull on the anchor, they think they are pulling the rock to themselves, but they are really pulling themselves to the rock.

This is what persistent prayer does. It pulls us closer to the Rock, God Almighty. As we move closer to God in prayer, we find that we do not get what we want from God. We get something better. We get what we need. We get what God wants. We find that as we move closer to our Rock, we begin to desire what God desires, so that what we ask for, knock for, and seek becomes what God so desperately wants to give us. The truth of Jesus' words comes to life so that what we pray for, we truly receive. It is a sacred surprise.

Are you still wondering about your unanswered prayers? God has an answer for you. But, whatever your request, know that God's answer will always involve your heart being changed by his love.

---

*Sermon aired on *Day 1* on September 18, 2005 (www.day1.net).

Chapter Four

I Wonder About God's Will For My Life*

We have all seen them. As we drive down the road, they are as plain as day. I am not sure who the source is, but they are certainly there — those signs from God on the highway. You know, the pitch black background with a white message from God. I saw one just the other day that read: "We need to talk — God."

I got to thinking about those signs and asked myself: Wouldn't it be nice if God really spoke to us this way? Wouldn't it be wonderful if we were ever confused about something, all we would have to do is look at a billboard and find the answer or look up into the sky and there would be something written in the clouds. Or what about the radio? That would be great! We could just tune in to a particular station each week and God's voice would break in and say, "This is what I want you to do."

A lot of us would love to hear from God in such a clear way. Then again, depending upon the message and the state of our lives, some of us would not! Overall, though, most people I speak with yearn to hear God's voice and want to know God's will for their lives.

God's will is one of the biggest issues I deal with as a pastor. People continually come to me, desperately wanting to know God's will. They often say, "I have a big decision, and I need to know what God wants me to do! I am at a crossroad, and I wonder what God's will is for my life." When I ask people what they would like to hear a sermon about, a frequent response is, "Finding God's will for my life." Obviously, finding God's will is important for many of us.

God's Will Is Not A Secret

I have great news! God wants us to know his will even more than we want to know his will. God's will is not a secret. Discovering God's will is not some kind of existential game of hide and seek during which God hides it and is amused by watching us try to find it.[1] God deeply desires for us to know and do his will.

Unfortunately, many have the notion that discovering God's will is reserved only for the spiritually elite. They hear friends speak about God as if he was at their breakfast table every morning, and then they wonder why they can't hear God, too. But being in tune with God's will for us is not complicated. All we have to do is know how to recognize his voice when he is speaking to us and then have the courage to do what he tells us.

Before we get into hearing and doing God's will, we need to have the right understanding of God's will. Many people have a false picture of God and how God views human beings. Instead of seeing God as loving and merciful, many see God as an angry, gray-haired old man with a stick, waiting to find those who are breaking the rules so he can punish them.[2]

Nothing could be further from truth! Read what the Bible says about God: 2 Corinthians 1:3 states that God is the Father of all mercies, and the God of all comfort. In John 10:11 we are told that God in Christ is the Good Shepherd who lays down his life for his sheep. 1 John 3:1 proclaims that God is the Sovereign God who loves us so much that he calls us his children. James 1:17 says that God is the Father who gives only good gifts.[3] The Bible is clear that we have a loving and merciful God.

The most convincing evidence for the good nature and will of God is God's revelation to us in Jesus Christ. God chose to reveal himself in Jesus Christ so we could understand what his nature is like. Through Christ, God communicated to us that he forgives us, loves us, and wants what is best for us — he went all the way to the cross to prove that to us!

What God Desires For Us

Romans 12:1-2 is clear about God's intentions for us. What God has in mind for us comes in three words in verse 2: "Good, acceptable, and perfect." God's will is good, acceptable, and perfect.

First, God's will is good. This means that God has the highest and best for us in mind. Second, God's will is acceptable. The Greek word for acceptable means "well pleasing" and "agreeable." Third, God's will is perfect, which means it meets the needs of the person.[4]

We can be sure that no matter what circumstance we face, we can have the peace that comes from knowing that God's will for us in any situation is good, acceptable, and perfect. God knows us better than we know ourselves, and he wants what is best for us.

We Have A Will, Too!

You may be asking, "Well, if God wants us to know his will, and it is good for us, why is it so difficult to discover?" The answer: We have a will, too! You see, often people know what God's will is for them; they just don't want to do it. They hide behind the statement, "Woe is me, I can't find God's will." In reality it is more like, "Woe is me, I don't want to do what God wants me to do."

There was once an agnostic who fell off a cliff. Halfway down, he caught hold of a bush. As he hung high above the ground, he shouted, "Is anybody up there?" Again, he shouted, "Is anybody up there?" A voice answered, "Yes, this is the Lord." The man yelled frantically, "Please help me!" There was a moment of silence. Then the Lord said, "Let go of the bush, and I will catch you." There was another long silence as the man looked at the ground far below. Then, he yelled, "Is anybody else up there?"

Haven't we done the same thing? We ask God to show us his will. We know in our hearts what he wants us to do, but we don't want to do it. Then we just hang there foolishly. Why do we do this? Pride. When out of control, pride can strip our spiritual gears and put us in a real mess. Pride is what started it all in the garden of Eden. Adam and Eve thought, "We don't need God; we can be gods ourselves." And we all know the pain and misery that followed. Too much pride can get us into a lot of trouble.

I saw this illustrated right before my eyes a few years ago. I was coming out of the church office, and I watched as a toddler got away from her mother and ran toward a busy street. The mother was pregnant and had an infant in her arms. I immediately dropped the books that were in my hands and ran after the child. I will never forget the look on the child's face. She looked back at me laughing, determined to outrun me, not knowing she was headed for great danger. Fortunately, I was able to catch her before she ran into the busy street.

Pride is like that. We get so filled with it that we are totally oblivious to where it is leading us. This is why it is impossible to live out God's will when we are filled with pride, for pride makes us stubborn to God's will, or it selfishly attaches conditions to God's will. It is almost comical. Our pride often causes us to bargain with God: "Yes, Lord I will forgive this person as long as he apologizes." Or, "Yes, Lord, I will serve in the church as long as I get recognized for my efforts." Is it any wonder that we have a tough time finding God's will and living it out when we live our faith in this way?

You see, doing God's will with certain conditions is not obedience. To obey and follow God's will means to surrender everything to God. God wants everything we are and hope to be. He wants all of us. So, if we are not surrendering to God, we are not obeying God.

Changing Our Approach To God's Will

C. S. Lewis once said that "all genuine religious conversions are blessed defeats." If we want to be clear about God's will and live it out, we must have a surrendered spirit. This means we must change how we approach God and his will for us. Instead of deciding what we want to do and asking God to bless it, we must decide to surrender all we are to God and ask him what he wants to do with us. We must put ourselves at the disposal of God. Then, and only then, will we be clear about our Lord's will for our lives. You see, if Jesus is really Lord of our lives, then he will rule every area of our lives. Remember, Paul says in verse 1 of chapter 12: "Present your bodies as a living sacrifice, holy and acceptable to God, which is your spiritual worship."

When I was a kid, I wanted nothing more than to please my dad. He would often show me how to throw a ball or swing a tennis racket or mow the lawn. As I did these activities, all I cared about was doing exactly what he told me. Each time I hit a ball or completed a task, I would ask incessantly, "How did I do? How did I do?" And the moment would come when he would put his arms around me and say, "You did great! I am so proud of you." I lived for those moments. That's all I cared about; pleasing my father.

May we have the same attitude toward our Heavenly Father. May we always be at the business of wanting to please God by doing his will. We hope for the day to come when we can ask God, "How did I do?" We long for God to respond, "Well done, my good and faithful servant." Let's live for that moment!

---

*Sermon aired on *Day 1* on September 25, 2005 (www.day1.net).

1. Eddie Rasnake, *Living God's Will* (Chattanooga, Tennessee: AMG Publishers, 2001), p. xvii.

2. *Ibid.*

3. *Ibid.*

4. *Ibid.*

Chapter Five

I Wonder About The Miracles In The Bible

Premarital counseling can be an adventure for pastors. You never know what two people filled with passion will say. I recall talking with a couple a few years ago about their upcoming nuptials. I was explaining to them the wedding ceremony. When I got to the reference of Jesus being at a wedding reception in Cana of Galilee and turning the water into wine (John 2), the soon-to-be groom interrupted me mid-sentence and asked, "You really don't believe that happened, do you? I mean, that sounds like a trumped up story, to me." He went on to say that he did not believe any of the miracles of Jesus actually happened.

I am sure you have been part of similar conversations. You have either been on the skeptical end or the believing end. And I am sure there are frequent times when you find yourself somewhere in the middle and ask, "I do wonder about the miracles in the Bible. Did they really happen?"

As you read through the Bible, you see miracle after miracle. Miracles are a significant part of Holy Scripture. In the book of Exodus, God rescues his people from bondage in Egypt through twelve dramatic plagues and by parting the Red Sea. In 2 Kings, Elisha feeds a poor widow and heals Naaman from leprosy. In the New Testament, the gospels tell us of a variety of miracles performed by Jesus. Many of the miracle stories of Jesus tell of the healing of those with physical ailments. In other cases, Jesus casts demons out of people suffering from spiritual or mental disorders. Three times we read that Jesus raised people from the dead, and the remaining stories reveal Jesus' power over things — like when he changed water into wine, fed a great crowd with very little food, walked on water, and calmed the storm.

There is no doubt that miracles are a significant part of the Bible. We must deal with them. As Christians, we don't take the part of the Bible we like and throw the rest away. We take the whole Bible, so we must take the miracles, too.

Do I believe the miracles recorded in the Bible really happened? Yes, I do. Now, I don't have irrefutable proof. I can't take you in a time machine and have you witness the miracles firsthand. But I tell you what I can do. I can tell you that I have firsthand experience with God. He speaks the truth to me over and over again in prayer and through scripture. I believe God when he tells me the truth about my life, so I should believe him when it comes to the miracles that he performed. Wondering about the miracles in the Bible is an issue of faith. If I trust God for my salvation, I should trust him about the miracles he performs.

The Purpose Of Miracles

If we choose to believe in the miracles of the Bible, then what should we believe about their purpose? Surely, there is more to miracles than just God impressing those who experience them. I believe miracles reveal the nature of God. They reveal his love, his priorities, his purposes, and his power. They give us a glimpse at the heart of God. For example, when we read about Jesus reaching out to heal those who are suffering, we see the grace, love, and kindness of God at work.

The miracles of Jesus were also performed so that we would come to believe that Jesus is our Lord and Savior. For instance, the reason John wrote about miracles was to lead us to believe that Jesus is the Christ and to have abundant life through him. John did not record the miracles of Jesus so we could say, "Wow, that's amazing!" like when we read a science-fiction novel. John wants us to respond, "Jesus is the Christ!" Miracles are not an end in themselves; they are a means to an end. We don't worship miracles. Miracles point to the Lord and lead us to worship him (John 20:30-31).

Do Miracles Still Occur?

A common question that needs to be addressed is, "Do miracles still happen?" Yes, I believe they do! God did not say, "I will perform miracles during this period of history and then stop forever." God is still active in our world today. Remember, God is not a static entity. God is always creating, always transforming, always moving among us and transforming us. Therefore, God is still performing miracles every single day.

The problem we have in our culture is that we like to separate unique events into two categories: natural/supernatural. If we can explain something scientifically, we don't think it is a miracle. But a miracle is any event that has God's power behind it. Life itself is a miracle! Medical doctors can explain the scientific process of childbirth, but this does negate the miracle of having a baby. Just ask mothers who have been through that experience. You cannot convince them that it was not a miracle. The miracles of God are all around us.

The *Sunday School Times* once published a story about an eastern king who was seated in a garden. One of his counselors was speaking on the wonderful works of God. The king said, "Show me a sign, and I will believe!" The counselor gave the king four acorns and said, "Majesty, plant these in the ground, and then stoop down for a moment and look into this clear pool of water." Then the counselor said, "Now, Majesty, look up." When the king looked up, he saw four oak trees where he had planted the acorns. The king said, "Wonderful. This is a work of God!" The counselor asked, "How long were you looking into the water?" The king said, "Only a second." The counselor replied, "Eighty years have passed as a second." The king looked at his garments and they were coming apart. He looked at his reflection in the mirror, and he had become an old man. The king said in anger, "Then there is no miracle here!" The counselor replied, "Yes, it is God's work, whether he did it in one second or eighty years." The miracles of God are all around us.

I am aware of what comes to some people's minds when they wonder about miracles. They want to know whether God can change something for them. They have a disease — they need money — they want an impossible event altered to make everything right again. They want a miracle! Well, I believe that God can and does perform these kinds of miracles. I cannot explain how and why these miracles happen, nor can I explain why some people are cured miraculously of a disease and some are not. But I believe we should pray for these miracles to occur. We should never limit God.

The Limitations Of Miracles

When we pray for miracles, we need to keep in mind one thing: Miracles are limited. For example, when Jesus raised Lazarus from the dead, Lazarus eventually became sick again and died. In addition, throughout scripture we observe that many who witnessed miracles did not end up following God. Amazingly enough, miracles do not always lead others to faith. This is just as well because miracles don't last and they don't ultimately save us. Only Jesus Christ can save us and give us eternal life.

When it comes to miracles, it is important to understand that there is a difference between a healing and a cure. A cure is a temporary solution. A healing is an eternal solution. A cure is a physical response. A healing is a spiritual event. A cure does not last. A healing lasts forever. A healing is discovering God's power within you to rise above any circumstance you face, even death!

If it comes down to a choice, I will take a healing over a cure, for a cure will only help one problem for a while, but a healing will give me the ability to cope and deal with any circumstance that comes my way. This is a true miracle: a life changed and empowered by God. In the end, this is what miracles point to: God's ability to transform us to live with his power and strength, no matter the circumstances of life.

The Greatest Miracle Of All

I recall visiting a lady in the hospital who was dying of cancer. Naturally, she was very sad and depressed. I took her hand at her bedside and asked God to work in and through her circumstance. I came back a few days later to discover that she was laughing with the nurses and enjoying the hospital meat loaf! She saw me and said, "I have been healed!" I asked, "What happened to the tumor?" "Oh, the tumor is still there," she replied. I was a bit confused. Helping me to understand, she said, "Pastor, I am enjoying every moment as a gift, and I am on my way to heaven to be with my Savior. Why shouldn't I be happy?"

That day I witnessed a miracle.

Chapter Six

I Wonder About The End Of The World

Of all the themes of our faith, what the Bible says about the end of the world ranks as one of the most controversial subjects. Not surprisingly, its controversial nature has also caused it to be one of the more popular subjects of our faith. Go into any Christian bookstore and you will see a plethora of books on the subject. These books contain as many opinions about it as there are books written about it. Turn on the television, and you will see preacher personalities touting their latest opinion about the end of the world. Some have elaborate maps and timelines and seem to be obsessed with the subject. We even have religious leaders try to predict the very day that the world will end. The day comes and goes and many well-intended people are simply left with lighter wallets and purses because they bought the books about these predictions. The obvious conclusion is that what the Bible says about the end of the world is misinterpreted and misunderstood.

Before we can come to a right understanding and perspective of this profound subject, we need to be formally introduced to it. I am going to throw you a big word: *eschatology*. The word comes from the Greek word, *esckatos*, which means "last." Eschatology literally means, "end times." Eschatology is the study of what the Bible says about final events and God's ultimate purposes for us and the world. You could also say that eschatology is the study of the destiny and conclusion of all the things that God has created, according to the purposes of God. Put simply, eschatology is about how God has designed the world as we know it to end.

God Is Going Somewhere

The study of eschatology is very important to our faith. Christians believe that God is working toward an end. We have a linear faith. God is working his purposes out so that the world as we know it with all of its sin, evil, and injustice will end, and the peaceful world he has intended will begin. This is what we mean when we sing the old hymn, "Marching To Zion." "We're marching to Zion, beautiful, beautiful Zion. We're marching upward to Zion, the beautiful city of God." The hunger and eagerness for this world to be transformed by God is expressed powerfully in Romans 8:19-25:

> *For the creation waits with eager longing for the revealing of the children of God; for the creation was subjected to futility, not of its own will but by the will of the one who subjected it, in hope that the creation itself will be set free from its bondage to decay and will obtain the freedom of the glory of the children of God. We know that the whole creation has been groaning in labor pains until now; and not only the creation, but we ourselves, who have the first fruits of the Spirit, groan inwardly while we wait for adoption, the redemption of our bodies. For in hope we were saved. Now hope that seen is not hope. For who hopes for what is seen? But if we hope for what we do not see, we wait for it with patience.*

God is transforming us and the world to become what he has wanted from the very beginning: a world in complete obedience to him. Another way we refer to this is the kingdom of God. The kingdom of God is where God reigns supreme. At this moment in time, God's kingdom both is and is not yet. We see bright glimpses of it, but it is not yet complete. Paul's words above express our deep yearning for God's kingdom to come and reign in all of its fullness.

Are We Left Behind?
Since most Christians yearn for the reign of God, you will find these deep yearnings expressed through many different views and opinions about how and when the world will end and God's complete reign will begin. We don't have to look very far to find someone who has an opinion on it. In fact, many would not believe how many different views and opinions there are about the end of the

world. When people are emotionally charged about a subject such as eschatology, it is inevitable that there will be intense debate about it. I will not go into great detail about these differing opinions and views, but suffice it to say that some are speculative, some are ridiculous, and some are just good fiction. There are many best-selling books out there that do a great job entertaining folks with graphic tales of the return of Christ, but they are not based on any serious scholarship of scripture. Most of them are based on a questionable approach to Bible study called *dispensationalism.* This approach to understanding the Bible is relatively new within the life span of the church, and it is not supported by church tradition.

Nevertheless, there are many Christians who diligently seek the Bible for answers about the end of the world. Some believe Christ will come before a tribulation and take away those who are saved and then come again later to receive those who are left. Some feel that Christ will come in the middle of a tribulation. Others are convinced that we have to suffer through a tribulation and then Christ will gather believers. There are those who call themselves "pre-millennialists." Pre-millennialists believe that Christ will come and reign on earth before the end of world and the last judgment. Others are "post-millennialists," and they believe that Christians will reign on earth first and then Christ will come again. Still, some call themselves "amillennialists," and they are convinced that there will be no 1,000-year reign, but the world will gradually convert and will finally be God's world. I am a "pan-millennialist." I believe it is all going to PAN out! I say this because Jesus specifically tells us that no one knows when the world will end, not even him! It is not our job to know:

> *But about that day or hour no one knows, neither the angels in heaven, nor the Son, but only the Father.*
> — Mark 13:32

We are not called as Christians to obsess about the details of the end of the world. We are called to be faithful. If we are obedient to God, we can be at peace with however and whenever God chooses to transform the world and establish the full reign of his kingdom.

Three Things Are Certain

Is there anything about the end of the world which is certain? I believe that there are three definitive facts that all Christians can agree upon when it comes to the end of the world as we know it and the establishment of God's kingdom.

First of all, we can be certain that *we will be transformed.* Throughout scripture we are promised that just as the world will be transformed, so will our bodies. We eagerly wait for the return of Christ and the redemption of our bodies so that the "earthly tent" we live in will give way to the heavenly dwelling the Lord has prepared for us. Our earthly bodies fail and decay, but our heavenly bodies will never pass away (1 Corinthians 15:51-54 and 2 Corinthians 5:1-2).

Second, when the world ends we can be certain that *we will be judged*. The Bible is consistent about the fact that there will be a time for God to judge each of us. Paul makes it clear: "For all of us must appear before the judgment seat of Christ, so that each may receive recompense for what has been done in the body, whether good or evil" (2 Corinthians 5:10). The distinction here is that it is not our sin that will be judged, but our actions, because we are forgiven by God in Christ. The judgment of God for those who are not Christians is another matter. As Christians, our sins have been taken care of through God's work of redemption in Christ. The key word Paul uses in the above passage is "recompense." Therefore, the judgment that Paul speaks of is about our faithfulness or lack of faithfulness being recognized by God. How we behave in response to being saved has eternal significance.

Third, when the world as we know it ends, we can be certain that *God will reign forever* (Revelation 11:15). There will be no more sorrow, suffering, or tears, only everlasting peace and joy as a result of God's glorious and infinite reign. There is an old story about an African-American preacher who was preaching to his congregation one Sunday morning. He confessed that when he was a child in school, he used to read the back of his textbook for the answers to his homework. Then he grinned, lifted up his black leather-bound Bible and shouted, "And I have read the back of *this* book and I know the answer. God wins! God wins!"

Be Ready

All of us must be ready for the full reign of God. We do not know how or when the world will end and God's complete reign will begin, but one thing we do know: We need to be ready.

Whenever I think of the moment of Christ's return and the complete establishment of God's kingdom, my mind harkens back to the days when I was in elementary school and our teacher would need to leave the room to retrieve something. She would tell the class to behave while she left the room for a few minutes. Of course, as soon as she was gone the class would go crazy. We would stand on the desks, throw things to each other around the room, and play "keep away" with people's lunches. But there was always someone in the room who would shout, "Y'all better get back in your seats and get quiet because the teacher is going to be back any second." We usually listened to this wisdom, and we were glad we did because none of us wanted to disappoint the teacher. Jesus said:

> *Therefore, keep awake — for you do not know when the master of the house will come, in the evening, or at midnight, or at cockcrow, or at dawn, or else he may find you asleep when he comes suddenly. And what I say to you I say to all: Keep awake.*
> — Mark 13:35-37

Chapter Seven

I Wonder About Life After Death

The assumption of this chapter is probably wrong. I have titled this chapter, "I Wonder About Life After Death," but the truth of the matter is that most of us typically do not wonder about death. Most of us choose to ignore the subject altogether. It scares us too much.

When I bring up the subject of death to people, I often get the reply, "Why would I want to think about that?" or "I don't want to think about that until I am old. I am young now and I will have plenty of time to think about that much later." I am impressed with the fact that people continue to think that they are invincible, that is, until they are confronted with their own mortality.

I recall going to a funeral home with a grieving family for a wake. One of the family members was a cancer doctor who faced death and dying quite a lot. However, he refused to be in the room with the open casket. When I caught up with him later and asked him where he had been, he replied angrily, "Life is for the living!" Even a cancer doctor could not deal with death.

Many people get very upset when the subject of death is mentioned. Some even get angry. In fact, some get so upset and angry about the subject that they virtually deny their own death. The denial of death is an interesting phenomenon in our culture.

The Fear Of Death

Why do we avoid the subject of death? Why do some people seem to be in denial about death? I believe our avoidance of the subject of death stems from the fact that death is a journey into the unknown. It is the ultimate mystery. We are afraid of those things that we don't understand and can't control.

To a degree, it is healthy to be afraid of death. It keeps us alive, and we need to have a healthy sense of caution for what we don't know. However, what is not healthy is to try to ignore our own death. All of us are going to die. There are no exceptions. As the old saying goes, "We don't get out of this world alive." We might as well face up to the fact that one day we will die. However, the fact we will die should not make us sad; it should make us grateful. Many of us see death as the great taker of life when actually the opposite is true; death is the great giver of life. As we struggle with the mystery of our death, we discover the meaning of our lives. Albert Schweitzer put the proper perspective on death:

> *We must all become familiar with the thought of death if we want to grow into really good people ... When we are familiar with death we accept each week, each day, as a gift. Only if we are able to accept life — bit by bit — does it become precious.*

Now, this is the right attitude about death! Death teaches us that life is a precious gift from God. If it wasn't for the fleeting nature of life, we would not love and appreciate it like we do. When we realize the preciousness of our time, we will make full use of our time. We cannot live life with courage, joy, and confidence unless we face the reality of our own death. In fact, "we cannot live fully unless there is something that we are willing to die for."[1] This is why the great Indian guru, don Juan, called death the "great ally."

If we choose to see the great things that death can teach us, death can become a very powerful friend. The beautiful irony is that once we come to accept death and what it teaches us, we truly begin to live. Why is there a cross before Easter? Why is there the crucifixion before the resurrection? Many Christians do not like to focus on Good Friday. They want to skip over it and go straight to Easter, but there is no Easter without the cross. We must go through Good Friday to get to Easter. There is no life without death.

What's On The Other Side?

Let us dive deeper into the great mystery of death and try to catch a glimpse of the other side. After all, the wonder of this chapter begs the question, "What happens to us when we die?" Obviously, we have limited information about what is on the other side for us, but within that limited information we have two strong sources: documented cases of near-death experiences and Holy Scripture.

Let me begin by touching on the compelling accounts of those who have had near-death experiences. Raymond Moody, a scientist and a psychiatrist who has extensively researched near-death experiences, reports that most of the people who remember their near-death experience relate a consistent account of the following events. First, they remember looking from above at their own bodies lying on a bed. Next, they are whisked through a dark tunnel of some kind, and when they come to the end, they are confronted by a beautiful light, which is usually perceived as God or Jesus. This being of light requires that they take a good look at what they have done with their lives. As they review their lives, they realize how much they have fallen short in living up to their potential, but the being is incredibly loving and forgiving. Then the being directs them to go back, and although they would much rather stay in the presence of the light, they reluctantly obey. The people who have these experiences come out of it with a commitment to make their lives matter, and with a firm belief in life after death. They also no longer fear death.[2]

Often I hear atheists criticize religion as a crutch for people who are scared of the mystery of death. I believe this is totally false. I don't believe that faith is a crutch; it is the truth. More importantly, atheists are the ones who are really scared. Most atheists like to downplay death as if it is no big deal. They deny the importance of it. The reality is that they are terrified to go beyond the surface and see the truth behind death. The truth is that behind the curtain of death for believers is a new dimension of life beyond our wildest dreams. What is beneath the mysterious surface of death is a loving, caring God with the answers to all of our questions, the fulfillment of all of our deepest longings, and the fruition of all God's great promises.

What The Bible Says About Life After Death

How do we know that life after death promises to be an overwhelming experience of joy for those who believe? The Bible tells us so. Let's take a look at what the Bible says about life after death.

Perhaps the most familiar passage of scripture that promises the gift of life after death is found in John 14:1-3. Here we find Jesus in the upper room comforting his disciples before his own death:

> *Do not let your hearts be troubled. Believe in God, believe also in me. In my Father's house there are many dwelling places. If it were not so, would I have told you that I go to prepare a place for you? And if I go and prepare a place for you, I will come again and will take you to myself, so that where I am, there you may be also.* — John 14:1-3

These are beautiful words that should comfort believers who find themselves apprehensive about death. This passage also reveals interesting aspects about life after death. For example, the phrase "dwelling places" could also be interpreted as "rest areas." In other words, these rooms are not permanent but provide respite. This implies that death is really a threshold to a whole new journey with God. On this journey we will be provided with comfort and rest along the way.

In addition to the passage in John, we find profound passages about life after death in the letters of Paul. If we had lived during the time of the Apostle Paul and we asked him what he believed about life after death, perhaps his answer would be what we find in 2 Corinthians 5:1-2:

> *For we know that if the earthly tent we live in is destroyed, we have a building from God, a house not made with hands, eternal in the heavens. For in this tent we groan, longing to be clothed with our heavenly dwelling.*

Later on in verse 5 of the same chapter Paul reminds us that God, who has prepared our heavenly dwelling, has given us the Holy Spirit as a guarantee of our extraordinary life after death.

Maybe the most compelling of Paul's words about life after death can be found in the fifteenth chapter of 1 Corinthians where

Paul reminds us that "if for this life only we have hoped in Christ, we are of all people most to be pitied" (v. 19). Paul's argument is clear: If there is no resurrection of the dead, then Christ has not been raised from the dead. If Christ has not been raised from the dead, then our faith means nothing (1 Corinthians 15:12-13). Paul's conviction leads us to the central promise our Lord gave us about life after death when he said, "Because I live, you also will live" (John 14:19).

We Are In Good Hands

As Christians we have nothing to fear from death. With Paul we know that "nothing can separate us from the love of God," especially death (Romans 8:38-39). We are promised that death is simply a journey into a deeper intimacy with God. Many have tried to explain the details of this mysterious journey. Some reflect on the relationship between our spiritual communion with God at death and the promise of our "earthly tent" being transformed into a "heavenly dwelling" with the return of Christ (2 Corinthians 5:1-2). Others take a more experiential approach and have sought to describe death like the experience of falling asleep as a child and a loved one putting you to bed. When you awake, you don't know how you got there, but you feel safe and secure.

The most profound attempt at explaining what we can expect from the mystery of death came from my colleague and friend, Ed Beck. When Ed was serving a church in Denver, he had a seven-year-old member of his congregation named Lynne who was dying of an incurable disease. Each time he would visit her in the hospital she would take him by the hand and lead him to other rooms to meet her friends. She was a very precocious child. A month before Lynne died he was visiting her and she said, "Reverend Beck, my mother told me to talk to you about dying. I don't want to die. Can you tell me what will happen when I die?"

Ed sat in a rocking chair and put Lynne on his lap and responded, "Lynne, before you were ever born you were in your mother's tummy, tucked away very near your mommy's loving heart. At that time, let's suppose someone had said to you, 'Lynne, you can no longer live in your mommy's tummy. It is time for you to die out of your mommy's tummy.' Now, Lynne, let's suppose you said, 'I don't want to leave my mommy's tummy. I love it here. It is nice and comfortable, and I feel very much loved in my mommy's tummy. I don't want to die out of my mommy's tummy. I don't want to be born because that means I'd have to leave my mommy's tummy.' " Ed continued and said, "But Lynne, you already know what happened. You did die out of your mommy's tummy and look what you discovered. You discovered in this world loving arms to hold you, loving faces smiling at you, and everyone wanting to meet your every need. And now for seven years you have discovered how wonderful it is to be out of your mommy's tummy. In fact, it is so wonderful that you don't want to die. You don't want to leave here. You don't want to leave here because you know you are loved by your mommy and daddy, your grandmas, your brother, and so many, many others, including me."

Lynne thought for a moment about the things Ed was saying to her. And then Ed said, "Lynne, there will soon come a time when you will die, and here is what is going to happen. The moment you die you will discover strong, loving arms holding you, loving faces smiling at you, and everyone will want to meet your every need. You will be surrounded by such love and beauty that soon, very soon you will say, 'I love it here. I don't want to leave here.' And Lynne, you won't leave. You will remain there and live with Jesus in heaven forever. Lynne, that is what is going to happen when you die." Then Ed concluded, "Oh, and one last thing. When you welcome me into heaven, take my hand and lead me from room to room so I can meet all your friends. Promise. Promise me you will do that. Promise!"

Jesus said, "I go to prepare a place for you" (John 14:2).

---

1. M. Scott Peck, *Further Along the Road Less Traveled* (New York: Simon and Schuster), p. 50.

2. *Ibid.*, pp. 60-61.

www.ingramcontent.com/pod-product-compliance
Lightning Source LLC
Chambersburg PA
CBHW061259040426
42444CB00010B/2424